THE PEOPLE'S BIRDS

ROBERT NORTHSHIELD

Foreword by David Brinkley

Charles Scribner's Sons   New York

125733

To the memory of L. E. Northshield,
who gave me my first camera
and many, many other things.

Contents

15

21

63

87

115

151

186

191

221

265

281

Foreword

I have never understood how Robert Northshield moved so easily to and from a superheated television news office in midtown New York and the distant, quiet, watery places where ducks fly and swans swim. Once his reflexes are tuned and adjusted to one, how can he stand the other? From extreme pressure to the extreme lack of it. Which of the two places is he escaping to? And from?

We all might ask ourselves the same questions. The emotional, intellectual, physical or even sensual satisfactions we pursue in our off hours—what are we really looking for? Sometimes, the answer is easy. One who spends the week swiveling around in a chair, moving back and forth but always remaining in the same place, might welcome a chance to use whatever muscles he has moving around on the weekend golf course. Most weekend golfers are easily seen to be weekend golfers, amateurs out there mainly for bonhomie and the mild exercise.

But Northshield is not easily seen as an amateur photographer of wildlife. He might actually be seen as a professional photographer of wildlife who in his off hours does vivid and imaginative work in television news. And two more disparate needs and drives must seldom be found in one man.

When he is at "work" he is busy with understanding and reporting to great masses of people the world of politicians and wars and other conflicts, and the world of humaneness and inhumanity and work and ambition and money and greed. Out there in those lakes and swamps, he is busy with the most beautiful pictures from pretty nearly the opposite end of the human experience. From the politician on the rostrum shouting, and perhaps lying, to the Canada goose on a cold lake honking his guileless truth, whatever it is.

Northshield makes it in both places, as far apart as they are.

We all snap a few pictures here and there and bore our friends with them. But few of us disappear from work for days and spend them sloshing around in cold water in Oregon or Alaska, usually alone, waiting for the snow geese to fly in, preferably at dawn so the early light will strike through their whitest wings and make them glow against the half-dark sky. Northshield does, and the results are in these pages—clean, bright and essential. They are pleasingly beyond understanding and beyond any need for it.

That may be it, though I am not sure. Those of us who, like Northshield, work at it all the time are sometimes terrified to think we truly do understand why the world of man and men is as it now is. But then we force ourselves to think about something else and get on with the work. I doubt that happens in an Oregon lake when the sun is rising.

DAVID BRINKLEY

I try to make pictures of emotions.

For many years, I have been a solitary watcher and listener and visitor. For fewer years, I have photographed what I felt.

Of course, I see more than I photograph. And I feel more than I see. I find that I must invest more emotionally in a picture than I do in just looking or memorizing. Making a picture means committing to the record the undeniable proof that I am not a collector of facts or a reporter; not an ornithologist or a photographer or an outdoorsman. Merely an anachronism: exultant in a time when the true chic is calm and cool and detached.

In recent times, I have relaxed a little. Now I photograph more of what I see and I see more of what I feel.

After long years of trying I have been able to attach myself to the camera without becoming anything more mystic than merely its owner and operator. I'm not its slave and it's not my soul; it has a job to do and, when directed properly, does it. I don't maltreat it, but I don't revere it. It's a machine that allows me not to be one.

Specifically, for those of us who are always bothering each other by asking about f-stops and film speed and things like that, I can describe my gear this way: I use two 35-mm. Nikon Photomic T cameras and I trust the exposure meters totally. One of the boxes has been adapted to use the Questar telescope. The other one is equipped with a motor drive that can whip thirty-six exposures in nine seconds. The first usually is coupled to the Questar or a 1,000-mm. Nikkor mirror lens on a sturdy (and really heavy) Linhof tripod. The motor-driven camera, on a shoulder brace, normally carries a 300-mm. Nikkor lens but I have a 50-mm. in my pocket.

I burn up fantastic quantities of Kodak Tri-X film, at a profligate ratio of about twenty exposures for each print made. I haven't been in a darkroom in about fifteen years. Professional magicians at the Berkey K & L lab in New York transform my images into contact sheets and then prints and I haven't any idea how they do it.

There is nothing private about the places I go; nothing private, but something special. Almost all of them are refuges owned and operated by the federal government, part of a system of 30 million acres, the largest in the world. They exist to protect and produce the fragile threatened billions of birds that form a part of the American experience. They exist to assure not only that there will someday be more than just seventy-five whooping cranes but also that hunters will have adequate millions of ducks and geese to shoot at. They exist to preserve the past and guarantee a future, and they work.

What makes them work well is the pleasant certainty that billions of birds migrate a couple of times a year. Nothing can stop the birds. Their mass movement is a massive stimulus: bird-eaters swarm out of their holes and dens and treetops, a tiny percentage with shotguns; bird-watchers of every degree of seriousness respond with scientific instruments and, more commonly, with bird books and notepads.

Generally, birds migrate to get where the food is or to get back to where the nest will be. The length of the journey, the miracle of navigation, the emotional drive are awesome. For me, they are a great convenience.

Canada geese

Black skimmers

Centuries of observation by generations of watchers are available to let me know where the birds are. That's where I want to be, in a different crowd, where, in Thoreau's words, ". . . he steps to the music which he hears, however measured or far away. . . ."

The music is of wings and cries. It's measured a hundred ways and not far away at all.

It has been heard on a window sill in Rockefeller Plaza when, surprisingly, a parula warbler peeped in at me and peeped away. And on a sand spit of Cape Cod, when a totally furious arctic tern dived and hit my son on the head and then returned to swirl at me and lay open a one-inch gash on <u>my</u> head, less thickly covered. And on a blustered plain in Texas, where thousands of big silver sandhill cranes blazed as they danced and fluttered and squawked. They were a

month and a thousand miles away from breeding and they were wild and strong.

The warbler, the tern, and the cranes were involved in raw emotional experiences. They shared them with me unwittingly, and I was able to respond and remember. That's what I like about birds and that's especially what I like about birds in migration.

When they migrate, birds of a species flock together . . . hugely. They don't take those long flights in a single leap but stop together to rest and wait and eat. Those way stations are well known.

They move, they react swiftly, they push to the limits of their endurance and our imagination; they emote. In their presence (if possible, in their midst), I can, too, and I do. Alone in this lovely crowd, I am, I believe, excused from intellectuality. I am permitted and even encouraged by myself to be emotional.

When the geese—whether they are Canada geese, white-fronted geese, cackling geese, Ross's geese, or snow geese—when the geese come whistling and wheeling onto Tule Lake, I need only feel and maybe react.

I need my hands only to shade my eyes, and my head only to calculate the difference in silhouette among Canada, white-fronted, cackling, Ross's and snow. I need not know where they came from or where they're going or whether I've seen them before or what makes them fly or why they're here or why I am. There is only one unavoidable fact:

They are beautiful.

One time, as I stood where all that beauty is, on the border of one of the National Wildlife Refuges in California, with bleary early-morning eyes I watched about a million geese and ducks pile into the sanctuary. The birds were everywhere, wedges of them crossing the sky and barely avoiding collisions, rafts of them hiding the surface of the marsh, mobs of them clogging the ditches.

There was a crusty hunting guide peering into the dawn with me and I told him that I thought the wildlife people do a marvelous job of conservation.

He didn't look away from the flights when he said, "They Goddamn well better. Them is the people's birds!"

What follows is a description of part of what happened to me where some of the people's birds are—where, hopefully, they will always be. ■

Black skimmers

The only way to approach Pelican Island is in a boat. It's a few hundred yards from the shore and it's too deep to wade and too far to swim if you want to bring cameras. What you should bring is a capacity for awe. Pelican Island, Florida, is a very important spot, the birthplace of a great American idea.

In 1903, by executive order of President Theodore Roosevelt, it became the first National Wildlife Refuge. Then, as now, if the tide is low and the wind is blowing right, the whole island manages to be just over three acres in size. The system that grew from that now includes 330 refuges, which comprise more than thirty million acres of the nation.

Those first three acres, Pelican Island, have been designated a National Historical Landmark and have been made a part of the National Wilderness System. All those capital letters show official government recognition but surely more impressive is the constant occupation of the island by brown pelicans . . . against heavy odds.

In 1910, a hurricane wrecked the place so the pelicans nested somewhere else. But they came back.

In 1918, the place was raided by misguided commercial fisherman who believed the birds were wiping out the ocean's fish. So they wiped out the young pelicans in their nests. The fishermen were stopped, the killings were stopped, and the pelicans came back again.

In 1924, the vegetation finally gave way under the weight of decades of nesting birds, so the pelicans needed another place to nest. They found one nearby but when the Pelican Island mangroves recovered, they made another comeback.

In 1970, there was another water shortage in the Everglades. In that endless train of man-made disasters, the results are often mysteriously visible far away. That time hundreds of wood ibises abandoned their dried-out rookeries at the southern tip of Florida and settled in at Pelican Island, 150 miles away on the east coast. The big invaders stabbed and ate dozens of nestling pelicans just after they were hatched. But some pelicans survived and the colony revived again.

For the past several years, the brown pelicans there have been studied and counted carefully. They are apparently healthy and certainly numerous, which is good news because brown pelicans, on a national scale, are on the way out. They've disappeared entirely from famous old nesting sites in California and Texas and Louisiana. Not due to hurricanes or irate fishermen or eroded land. The brown pelican is an endangered species because of the persistence and indiscrimination of chemical pesticides that invade the oceans and their fishes and the birds that eat them. This makes for thinning of the shells of eggs and that fragility adds up to genocide.

So far, some thinness has been detected in the eggshells on Pelican Island, but the young birds are still being hatched in large numbers. The population has remained constant for many years and it can be deduced that feeding in the Atlantic is less harmful to pelicans than eating fish in the Gulf of Mexico or the Pacific. But there is DDT everywhere and when it's inside pelicans they are horribly threatened. In time they may disappear from Pelican Island.

For now, they crowd the place and make it important.

The welcome to Pelican Island is beautifully frightful. At the approach to their nesting place, the birds, a couple of hundred of them, sprang up and flew directly toward us and over the boat. The sky was filled with flapping giants that looked in silhouette like a flock of pterodactyls. But the only sound was of wings and wind because adult pelicans are mute.

Right at the edge of the island was a nest with a day-old bird, another hatching out, and one unhatched egg. The nestling, the only young bird I saw that day, peeped and squawked. The refuge manager, Lawrence Wineland, told me soon it too would become as silent as its parents. It is theorized that salt water feeding destroys the birds' voices. The island would be a deafening place otherwise. Almost every square foot of foliage is filled with birds, their nests and droppings and leftover fish.

On that hot January morning, it had the terrible smell of fervent life I've found in so many crowded, wondrous places. The odor makes my eyes water and my nostrils contract and my mouth smile. Being in a mobbed rookery is somehow like being in the nucleus of an enormous cell, where all the meaningful stuff of life is going on without rest and with a wonderful rhythm.

Brown pelicans and black vultures

Nesting had begun around Christmas and would peak in February. There would be nests and eggs and young birds until September, but now they were still building and breeding. There were a great many eggs, always three to a nest, and probably quite a few new pelicans although we saw just that one bare red baby.

There were about a thousand brown pelicans. There were also a dozen nests of great blue herons (with the huge waders standing guard or sprawling on them or improving them with more twigs), and several dozen cormorant nests.

Fish crows and boat-tailed grackles screamed from the mangrove bushes. A few white ibises glided in and some wood ibises and anhingas carried small branches to start their nests. At one side of the island, there were ten or fifteen black vultures silently perched, waiting for something to die, waiting for that inevitable product of so much life.

In the shoals around the islet there was a thick white circle of birds: flocks of ring-billed gulls and herring gulls, royal terns and Caspian terns, American egrets and snowy egrets and, spectacularly, white pelicans, nearly twice the size of their brown relatives. They are migrants to Florida, winter visitors from the northern part of the Great Plains, thousands of miles from their nesting places, building up their bodies in readiness for mating a month away.

And above us, wheeling, soaring, searching, a bald eagle and a magnificent frigatebird.

The island is sand. The black mangrove and the red, separate species (but indistinguishable to me), cover it but not completely. Years of living with thousands of big birds have reduced the height of the plants to about five feet and many of them are broken and bent, so there is space to travel easily among the bushes. There are a few puddles and, in season, mosquitoes and chiggers to make it adventurous. But generally it is a pleasant, easy place to make pictures. I exposed nearly five hundred in an hour and a half.

I photographed a great many birds but not nearly all those that were there. My near approach to a nest put them up but they always came back. I could get to within ten feet before they flew away, and backing off just a yard was all the enticement they needed to return. That's pelicans.

The great blue herons were a little more skittish and the double-crested cormorants were most shy. That, said Lawrence, is because they were still in the early stages of nesting. By the time they had hatched their young, their commitment to home and its defense would be more profound. They'd stay longer, their reaction would appear to be more thoughtful: not blind flight but parenthood.

own pelican (soaring), great blue heron (left) and wood ibis

Black vultures, brown pelicans and (opposite) nesting great blue herons

Great blue herons, white pelicans, brown pelicans, double-crested cormorants and a wood ibis

Just two weeks later, luckily in Florida again, I got back to Pelican Island for a few more hours. This time it was crowded with nervous parents and nests filled with bawling, scrawny babies. The adult birds stayed at the nests longer now and didn't spring away until we got within a yard or so.

Their absence revealed every stage of hatching and early growth. There were still many eggs intact, some with the first hole pecked through and showing the tips of tiny bills and a great many more abandoned and useless around fully born pelicans or cormorants. Very young great blue herons peeked over the edges of their high nests as they crouched with an instinctive appreciation of defensive action.

We watched peckings and hatchings and feedings and even some impossible attempts at wing-flapping performed by pelicans grotesquely large after only two weeks of life.

New nesters, ibises, anhingas, egrets and even more brown pelicans, glided in to work.

And this is the place they come, all these species, to build a hopeful future for their kind. All around Pelican Island there are other seemingly identical little spots of green in the shallow water. But this is the home to which they come and stay and breed and produce and die and we need them, the birds and the place.

Brown pelican, age about ten minutes

Two brown pelicans with a third on the way and (opposite) three double-crested cormorants

Brown pelicans, age two weeks

Adult brown pelicans and (opposite) immature pelicans

The brown pelican used to be famous in Louisiana. The people there called it the Pelican State. They even had a delightful little pelican cartoon on their automobile license plates. Now the pelican is gone from the plates because it is gone from Louisiana. Totally and permanently.

So Lawrence Wineland led a little expedition to his island refuge recently to capture five brown pelicans. They were shipped to the New Orleans zoo so that Louisiana school children could know what their state bird looks like.

That's what an endangered species is. A big, beautiful thing, well-fed, cared for, nursed and displayed in a large, airy cage. But that's much different from that cloud of pterodactyls springing silently from nests into a flawless sky, digging into a wind that whistles their huge wings, circling back to their ancient home where they belong. ■

It was the first decent day of miserable March, a Sunday, when the rain stopped and the sun shone and the battered reeds showed strength enough to stand up straight. Winter still was here, but this was a little holiday, full of the promise of warmth. The woods willingly revealed some crocuses and skunk cabbage where the ground was wet and partly thawed.

Along the reservoir, cars sped and slid on last night's ice. The water swept up almost to the road and carried very old leaves and branches into the tangle of the rushes, tan and drab, but seeming to show some opposition to the water's force. I saw some blackbirds and a few mallards; there were plenty of winter birds still flying and fussing: juncos, jays, chickadees, a pair of cardinals, mourning doves challenging the cars on the shiny pavement. And I saw a mute swan.

It was big and white and immaculate. No major discovery this, but for me it was a small miracle because I had never seen a swan here before and because it had been so long since I had seen anything to reassure me that renewal would happen. (Just before each spring, I really doubt that I'll ever see another long day or a warm one or one filled with wakefulness and growth.)

Although it was late in the day and I could make only a few pictures before dimness capped my lens, I could see that the swan was searching and planning, scratching and pulling to put together a nest. The possibilities were spectacular.

The next day, driving to the city through the rain, I detoured past the reservoir and, pushed by loud and insolent horns, was able only to slow a little to look. It was enough: in the foggy green-gray there were two big swans busy on a pile of twigs and branches, and the future was assured.

March, the lion of tradition, roared into April and into a busy, terrible time. I know that the swans and I were part of the world as it changed and grew but we didn't see each other. Before I got back to the reservoir again, this happened and more:

FROM THE HUNTLEY-BRINKLEY REPORT:
APRIL 1-5, 1968

. . . The President is waiting for Hanoi's response to the reduced bombing he announced last night . . . and the country's political hierarchy is waiting for the shock and confusion of last night to settle down. Late last night and most of today, the prominent politicians—candidates and otherwise—were poking around for something seemly and appropriate to say about President Johnson's refusal to run again . . . and about its effect on themselves. Most of them didn't find much to say, other than polite generalities. And the American political scene is still in a state of confusion.

. . . North Vietnam says it is now willing to meet representatives of the United States . . . and to discuss the complete, unconditional stoppage of the American bombing of the north . . . so talks can then begin. President Johnson promptly said he was very interested.

. . . In South Vietnam today . . . about 20 thousand Allied troops are pushing through to Khe Sanh, the outpost held by five thousand Marines and now accessible only by air.

. . . There were no stunning surprises in the Wisconsin primary; but there were portents and signs and meaningful implications. The Democrats gave 57 per cent of their ballots to Senator Eugene McCarthy, 35 per cent to President Johnson; and 6 per cent of them laboriously wrote in the name of Robert F. Kennedy. McCarthy won 52 of the delegates.

. . . Memphis city officials went into federal court again today to try to prevent a Negro mass march on Monday. The Ku Klux Klan reportedly is planning a countermarch and police testified they will be unable to prevent violence. Dr. Martin Luther King has planned the march in support of striking garbage collectors. He spoke at a rally last night.

. . . President Johnson has ordered Federal troops moved in to protect Washington. There was substantial arson and looting last night . . . and it started again today. Smoke from burning stores drifted over the downtown area and over the dome of the United States Capitol.

. . . The body of Martin Luther King, Junior was returned today to Atlanta . . . where he was born . . . from Memphis . . . where he died last night.

. . . There have been massive demonstrations of grief in many cities. Most of them have been peaceful. But, in at least 25, the protests have been accompanied by violence and arson. Schools have been closed, office workers have been sent home, extra police and firemen called to duty. There have been four deaths, all of white people. Several people, Negro and white, have been wounded by guns or knives. Others have been injured; at least 50 in New York City alone. There have been hundreds arrested, most for looting.

For six weeks, through that cruelest month and through half of May, as a producer of television news programs, I had seen and heard and felt the world. Now, home from Milwaukee and New York and Indianapolis and Paris, I rested at the reservoir.

I knew that one day, suddenly, the fat willow buds had become thin yellow leaves; that one day the swans pressed and beat together, their pulses racing, their bills clacking, their eyes gleaming. That the female had lifted up from the nest, away from seven eggs where there had been nothing but a messy pile of moss and twigs and wet black leaves.

One day there was no more ice and the snapping turtle pushed up through the mud and, still sleepily, grabbed and ate a frog in dull remembrance of what living is. And on another day, seven cygnets, knowing nothing, using close to all the strength that had been only yolk and albumen a few weeks before, gripped by the strongest determination they'd ever feel, one day had broken their shells and were mute swans.

On those days and others among them, there were new great horned owls in an oak near the water, new perch and sunfish among the bright new water grass roots, new warmth and clouds and winds and violence very old.

To be lazy and purely absorbent, to do nothing more constructive than look through a telephoto lens and push a button from time to time, is to forget that there is a Memphis or a Washington and to know only that where there were two beautiful birds there are now nine. There are strong intimations of immortality. It is easy to see things that aren't there.

What was there was this: a family of swans, idyllic, providing a cliché of peace and simplicity. No shock but one—sometimes I thought the seven young had become six, only to discover, ridiculously, that one was riding on its mother's back.

Through a couple of weeks of early mornings, I saw the cygnets learn to paddle around and finally to swim: that strong, surging glide of impressive velocity characteristic of full-grown swans. I watched the parents teach them how to tip to eat, which grasses are the right grasses, how a nest is built. I wasn't there to see the preflight and flying lessons but those, too, must be taught.

Toward the end of May, the family appeared snugly secure. No curious ducks or geese came close to the hissing protective parents. The swans swam only along the most obscure borders of the pond, far from fishermen and young hunters.

I saw them huddle on their old nest at sunset one evening and left the next day for where my work was, this time in California.

FROM THE HUNTLEY-BRINKLEY REPORT:
JUNE 5-7, 1968

. . . Senator Robert F. Kennedy was shot in the head and gravely wounded early today before hundreds of people in his political headquarters in a Los Angeles hotel . . . seconds after he made a speech celebrating his victory over Senator Eugene McCarthy in the California Democratic Presidential primary. Tonight, he lies unconscious in Good Samaritan Hospital in Los Angeles.

. . . In the anguish and weariness of the long night and long day, there were many who recalled what a friend of President Kennedy's had said after the assassination: "The time will come. We will laugh again, but we will never be young again."

. . . It is impossible to conclude anything sensible from a totally senseless act . . . as it is impossible to be rational about the irrational. Because the two are on separate levels of being . . . so far apart there is no real communication between them. But the results of senselessness and irrationality are a part of our lives.

. . . At 1:44 this morning, Pacific time, the life of Senator Robert F. Kennedy ended, 42 years after it began, and 25 hours after he was felled by an assassin.

. . . However much Americans dislike it and disown it . . . violence in many forms, including political murder . . . is a part of the life of our country. Senator Kennedy is the latest victim. No one can say he is the last.

. . . The funeral will be tomorrow. A requiem mass . . . then a train ride to Washington . . . where the Kennedy family will travel a route they have traveled before . . . over the river to Arlington. There, Senator Kennedy will be buried beside his brother, and he will leave behind:

A vacant seat in the United States Senate.
A campaign for President, ended in the middle.
A hundred-odd Presidential delegates pledged to him, who must vote for someone else.
And a big staff, including many who quit their jobs to work for him.
A mother and a father who have seen one daughter and three of their four sons die violently, two of them murdered.
One wife.
Ten children, and one more yet unborn.
And a country outraged at the viciousness in its midst and wondering what will come next.

A few hours after televising the funeral in Arlington, I was back at the reservoir. I sought nothing more significant nor mysterious than some quiet and some beauty. These I found.

Had I sought some symbols of solace or reassurance, I would have forced myself into an argument. For there were the swans. They still glided perfectly and posed gracefully, and they seemed assured and secure. The cygnets were a little whiter, rough instead of fluffy, bigger and more like swans. When I had last seen them, there were seven.

Now there were four.

Surely three had died violently; there is almost no other way for a young swan to die. Probably one of the great horned owls had glided onto the nest pile, its efficient stereoscopic eyes finding the young bird, silently, quickly grabbing it, winging it to the oak where young owls ripped with a hungry frenzy.

Or the snapping turtle, floating up through the blackness, snatching at a paddling webbed foot, drowning the bird and dumbly devouring it. Or a red-tailed hawk that I've seen often, waiting intelligently on a high-tension tower. Most likely a raccoon. Maybe a fox or a skunk. But surely, necessarily, by violence.

Confusion, simple and great, was possible here. I could have argued that the swans were a solid token of safe reality. Then the death of the three would show that nothing is good, nothing is as it should be.

Or I could conclude that the loss of the young birds had no meaning, cosmic or prosaic.

Or I could accept what was obvious: there were two adult swans and four young ones and all of them were beautiful and entertaining. To demand more of birds is ridiculous.

By now the young birds were nearly white, nearly half the size of the adults. They still swam together and foraged under water together, but the parents seemed less attentive, more at ease when the young swans traveled apart and tried bold plans. For these weeks of summer, there was nothing more to teach. The cygnets could do everything but fly.

Now June was through and July nearly so. Everywhere in the country demands were made to put an end to violence. It was new and bad and unnatural, we were told, and violence must be stopped. I left the swans in their tranquil place and headed for Miami Beach and Chicago to learn the plans of those who would legislate us out of violence.

FROM THE HUNTLEY-BRINKLEY REPORT:
AUGUST 8-30, 1968

. . . NIXON SOUND ENDS: "I have made a
decision I shall recommend to the convention that it nominate for Vice President on
the Republican ticket Governor Agnew of
Maryland."
. . . Senator Eugene McCarthy said the
Presidential race between Nixon and Vice
President Humphrey would not offer the
voters a clear choice.
. . . Antiwar demonstrators have been
threatening to lead a march of 10 thousand
people to the convention hall. Today several thousand of them gathered in Grant
Park, in downtown Chicago, planning to
walk the five miles from there to the
International Amphitheatre. There was at
least one scuffle with police when a hippie
tried to pull down an American flag and the
police stopped him. Police moved in with
night sticks and restored order, but the
situation remained tense. Last night there
was more violence in Lincoln Park.
. . . So, as night falls here in Chicago,
it would seem that the stage . . . for
trouble . . . is set and waiting. Almost
12 thousand protesters are in Grant Park--
right now. And between the park and the
convention hall . . . waiting to meet them
. . . are five thousand National Guardsmen, 75 hundred Regular Army troops, and
12 thousand Chicago policemen. Just minutes
ago, some of these protesters tried to
start the march but were stalled almost
immediately by police and Guardsmen.
. . . Vice President Humphrey now is the
Presidential candidate of the Democratic
Party . . . but even as he admitted . . .
his happiness is far from complete. The
Vice President was nominated last night at
a convention riven by deep disagreement in
the party and accompanied by widespread
violence outside the convention hall.
. . . Mayor Daley and the Chicago police
have been criticized . . . and defended
. . . for their performance in the streets
here last night. The Mayor issued a statement saying a few policemen may have over-
reacted . . . but in general he said they
used only what force was necessary when
the demonstrators attacked them. A Police
Department spokesman said about the same
thing . . . and said the press and television had mounted a propaganda campaign
against the police.

I rested for a couple of weeks in the wilderness
of Wyoming and Utah before going home. I didn't get
back to the swans until mid-September. But even after
all the shocks, 1968—that slum of a year—still held
another small one: where there had been seven young
swans, then four, now there was but one.

The swans glided around the lake, all three of them the same size, as the days shortened and the mornings chilled. One day I photographed them. The next day, driving to the sleety city, I found them gone.

Missing, too, were any errant thoughts about the evils of violence. For the swans had simplified everything for me: there is an important, pervasive, overlooked difference between violence and destructiveness. We waste our time and dissipate our will by ranting and bemoaning about violence. Instead, we should, I think, learn what it is, accept the natural, and force the unnatural into the dark corner of rejection.

And we should recognize that destructiveness is often silent, calm, penetrating but non-violent.

In that year, many ideas and feelings were destroyed without any show of violence. Ideas died in those heads ripped apart by bullets, but what mattered is that the ideas died, not how it happened. Ideas died in Lincoln Park and in Saigon and in voting booths that year, too. And mercury and pesticides and ignorance and hatred seeped into ponds and streams and livers and brains and it was utterly non-violent.

As for that family of swans, now only three, winging south together: now, at the end of a long season of true violence, there were three where there had been two.

On April 16, 1969, I noted in a little black book that three mute swans had appeared at the reservoir.

By April 22, a fourth had arrived and it was apparent that they were arranging themselves into pairs. ■

In late September, on the northern coast of Alaska, on the tundra of the Yukon and the Northwest Territories, on the muskeg and dreary marshes north in Alberta and Saskatchewan, the days shorten dramatically. The food has begun to hide and the pack ice has stiffened. The ponds have a greasy cover of frozen gray. The ducks and geese, millions of them, get the urge.

It is time to move.

Like the millions before them, over millions of years, they coo and puff and stir about and, at last, singly, in pairs, and in families, spring upward into the sharp edge of wind. This is the end of a cycle or the beginning of another. The birds are propelled into the northern twilight by nothing more sophisticated nor less important than the need to survive.

The enormous area of Canadian and Alaskan wilderness provided long warm days in spring and summer, and food and safety and nesting places for all the birds and more. Now the pairs that came up in spring are families and the days are short and dark. The future lies to the south. So, in little V's, in sloppy wedges and graceful curves, they wing out of the hungry north.

There is no way—and little need—to know how long the ducks and geese have known about Klamath Basin. No doubt the warm marshes along the California–Oregon border have attracted them ever since the last glacier retreated. For just over sixty years, it's been official.

The first National Wildlife Refuge for waterfowl—that at Lower Klamath—was established by President Theodore Roosevelt in 1908. Three years later, another was set aside at Clear Lake. In 1928, Tule Lake was established and others at Upper Klamath and Klamath Forest have been added to make a complex of five that serves as a locale for one of the last great spectacles. Here, in October and November —every October and November—is the greatest concentration of waterfowl in the world.

There are sure to be five million pintails, half a million mallards, a quarter of a million widgeons and teal, shovelers, scaup, ruddy ducks, and common mergansers in the hundreds of thousands. There are more than a quarter of a million each of white-fronted geese and Canada geese (including four sub-species) and nearly that many snow geese. Most of these are restless hordes on the move. There are 160 different kinds of birds that nest on the 120,000 acres of the refuges, but many of them have moved south by the time the northern myriads come cackling in. Most of the 80,000 ducks and geese produced each year in the basin stay to mingle with the birds from the north.

There are remnants, flashy and impressive, of the breeding colonies of gulls and terns and cormorants and white pelicans and a dozen species of shorebirds. There are cranes and eagles and hawks and dozens of the singers and chirpers that can be seen wherever there's a shred of wildness.

But the reason to move to Klamath is to see those unbelievable flocks that have also found a reason to move.

The absolute population peak of ducks is reached in mid-October, just when the hunting season begins. There are as many as eight million birds in the Klamath Basin then and, from the sound of the shooting, there seems to be a like number of hunters. Two weeks earlier, when there are a mere two million ducks and geese, there are no shotguns, no sounds but wind and wings and quacking and gaggling and honking . . . a lovely, wild, tuneless glare of life.

My first visit to the area was on one of those cool early October mornings. For a full eight hours I stayed in one spot on the edge of a Lower Klamath pond. It was much too early for the big flocks of geese, I was told. They and their hunters mass in early November, I was told. But I stayed, and saw a display of white-fronted geese that had no parallel in my experience.

They came into the water and moved out from it at every angle, every altitude, on azimuths and elevations to confound a geometry professor.

Like all geese, they are stately and handsome. People who know them better than I call them "laughing geese" or "specklebellies" or "specks." I had always felt, on the basis of my seeing them only in the pages of bird books, that such names were inaccurate and vaguely disrespectful. But to spend some hours watching is to learn enough to build an amused affection.

They <u>are</u> stately and handsome, as they V high over a field or across a stony cliff. But when they call, they giggle. Their cry is like the laugh of a happy drunk or the creak of a comfortable old chair and when they move toward the water to loaf or into a barley field to gorge, all laws of aerodynamics are suspended.

A single flight of ten geese is apt to have three fly in magnificently, like proper big birds, and a couple float down till the last moment and then drop clumsily to the water, and two or three more flap around and squawk and sound alarms that have no cause, and the rest do outlandish acrobatics that include complete flipovers and sideswipes. The courtly mien is reassumed immediately upon landing, when they stand or swim in even rows, their slender necks vertical, their striped bellies pouty.

Pintails (at top), California gulls and white-fronted geese

While I looked at the geese, there were other diversions. Flocks of white pelicans floated along the edges of islands or ponderously ran and flapped along the water to get into the air. They beat and circled steadily to find strong currents and rode them upward to soar, clean white sails against the brilliant blue.

Avocets

Pintails

A little flock of avocets, with upcurved bills tucked securely under their wings, loafed along a mud bar thirty feet beyond me. At a handclap, they flipped their heads around in a marvel of synchronization and gave me a profile as they faced into the heavy breeze.

A few American egrets, large and white, waded silently in the very shallow water. Coots scooted among them and into the rushes on the shore.

There were grebes floating with grace and charm, fixing me with their disproportionately huge red apple eyes. There were ducks, busy and noisy, and there were great blue herons pacing about and piercing food.

97

But mostly that day there were geese. For periods of twenty minutes or so it was not possible to look around without seeing a wedge or a skein of them moving toward the water. There were times when nothing seemed to move, noisy times when flocks and sub-flocks all over the pond suddenly flapped off to circle and set again no more than fifty yards from where they'd lifted. Best was the late afternoon. The clouds, which had made a spectacle of their own all day, broke up and moved over to one side of the sky. A sharp light from the southwest ran the same direction as the strengthening wind, straight into the flocked white faces of the geese.

They glared for a few minutes and then, by tens and hundreds, on wings that whirred and whistled and made the air pulse, they lifted up and disappeared over the ridge. Ten thousand had been where now there was none. They had made their loud move in less than three minutes.

White-fronted geese

99

One day at Klamath Basin there were almost no snow geese. The next day there were hundreds. The day after, many thousands. Each night I heard them honking and squawking over my motel and each morning I saw them bunched on Tule Lake and erupting into the air when I got too close. They were more stunning than I had anticipated.

Snow geese lack the dignity and power of the big Canadas. They aren't as amusing as the white-fronted. But they have a benign look and shape that is pleasing and somehow gentle. They are hardy and strong and drive through the air with great purpose, but at rest they seem symbolic of tranquillity. When I stopped my car and stepped out to photograph them, a flock of thirty or so just turned their tails toward me and paddled slowly away. No alarm, no panic.

But when more aggression from me put them up, their black-tipped wings pulled them off the water with awesome power and speed.

Through the days that I watched them, the snow geese became ever more plentiful. When there were just a few, they swam and flew together. Often my being there put them into the air, where they'd hover or move away slowly.

Against a beige mountain background, their name
took on meaning. They are called snow geese, no
doubt, because they are white. But treading air, wings
beating fast, with the sun blazing off their feathers,
they look like an isolated snow storm, each bird a flake,
the flock shimmering and shivering.

When more of them arrived from the far Arctic,
the marsh and ponds were too crowded for isolation.
Large rafts of birds formed and when they took off
in a spectacle of cries and fury, the integration was
obvious. There were white-fronted geese, Canadas,
and their small relatives the cackling geese, and
among them all were the shiny snow geese.

Snow geese

Klamath Basin in the fall is cloudy with ducks. They leap from every ditch and dike and come quacking in and out of the fields of millet and barley. They lace the sky with their dark lines. In the two-and-a-half-month hunting season, more than 70,000 of them are killed. It doesn't seem to make a mark in the vastness of the flocks.

Most of the ducks, like most of the geese, come to Klamath from somewhere else each fall. Large numbers breed and nest and hatch on the five refuges, but far more migrants come to rest and feed en route from north to south. In the spring and summer, ducks can be seen and known as individuals or pairs or families. But in the autumn they are part of an immense mass that seems to be a gigantic animal, with each bird a single cell. The sights and sounds are huge. Wingbeats are a roar and the crying of the birds an enormous envelope.

It is no time for peaceful contemplation of courting drakes and their coy mates; it is a time of drama, a time to be engulfed by strong, eager creatures that move massively.

Ducks: pintails, mallards, widgeons

The joy of those five refuges in the fall is in the waves and layers and fogs of birds, the tumult of thousands. But everywhere there are also vignettes. Small scenes of wilderness, the tiny plays without scripts that are routine but never common.

Late one afternoon, my last one there, the autumn sun did again what it had done each day: it etched its way through day-old banks of clouds to shine on the nearly-white fields of barley. In one plot, I saw the heads of a few sentinel geese watching while a good-sized flock fed. I got out of the car to walk closer and photograph the darkly-silhouetted birds. As I moved, so did a band of five mule deer. They pranced out of a deep ditch and through the barley. Suddenly they ran, and the geese exploded from the grain field. It was a short, vibrant scene of honking, wing-whirring motion. I got a few pictures.

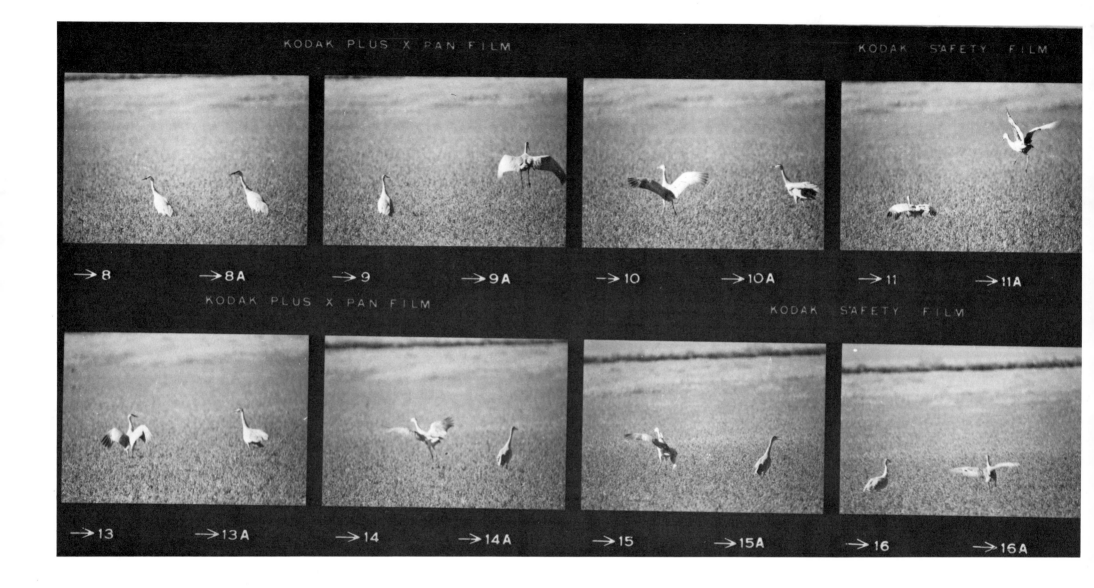

12 12 A

17 17 A

Even later, I was guided to another field where sandhill cranes were known to feed. I had never seen one and I wanted to. In fading light, I came upon them unexpectedly, eagerly. I made as many pictures as I could in the half minute between my arrival outside the car and their departure across the prairie.

For thirty seconds, I was an excited part of their dancing, leaping wildness. (I have sought it and found it many wild times in many wild places since.)

"In wildness," wrote Thoreau, "is the preservation of the world."

It is there, in the Klamath region, where it has always been.

It is there and when spring and its birds inevitably returned, it would again be time to move. ■

Okefenokee looks like what people expect the Everglades to look like. In fact, Okefenokee looks like nothing else but Okefenokee. Unique. Endless, it seems, and indestructibly green, lush, powerful, eerie, successful, peaceful but teeming with countless skirmishes. There are so many different kinds of plants and animals, with so many varied appetites, that there are millions of meals being contemplated or consumed in the swamp all the time. The alertness born of either fear or hunger is palpable.

The immense swamp, about 750 square miles of it, is as it always was, ever since the Okefenokee was born in the Pleistocene. The mission of the men who manage the federal refuge is simply to keep it that way.

So among the intimations of primordial wilderness, you can glide along the fabled Suwannee River on the western side of the swamp (there's no place to walk) and be aware of life and time before there were people. Everything seems harmonious although there is great clashing of colors, although the screams and buzzings and splashing have no rhythm, although the smells of fish and algae and flowering vines and evergreens overlap. But it works, efficiently, neatly, pleasantly. There is enough of everything and everything is used to make it beautiful.

You cannot escape the feeling that you are being watched all the time in the great cypress bogs and the wet prairies. What was certainly a half-submerged log slithers into the black water and reveals itself as a big alligator; the shiny rock splashes in to show that it's a turtle; the dead leaves in a crotch of a tree show two wet eyes and become a staring raccoon. A vine is really a snake, the little plants are beetles, the resting butterflies actually are flowers. The swamp is a complex system of life where thousands of diverse species, surrounded by their enemies, all survive.

And as you glide and try to be alert to all the life, as you watch, you are watched, too. Apart from all the bizarre reptiles, and the skittering insects, the bears and bobcats and opossums, apart and usually above, there are birds.

Wood ibises

Wood ibises

I have toured Okefenokee several times, once in winter. That time it was warm and green but I saw almost no birds: a half-dozen egrets, a few buzzards, about ten red-shouldered hawks in six hours of boating. Everything else was about the same but the absence of birds made it seem dead, deserted.

More than two hundred bird species live in the refuge. A great many of them are hugely visible, often raucous and showy. Some wade and wallow, expertly and endlessly spearing frogs or minnows or digging up crustaceans. Some fly singly, remarkably, along narrow channels in the trees and some move in big flocks just above the forest. In season, all of them seem to be busy building big and obvious nests though there are others, of course, that do nothing but fight their way out of eggs and pant and gasp in their earliest experience of life.

What's wonderfully different about the birds of Okefenokee is that they all seem to pose for their pictures. They seem unaware of any need for camouflage or subterfuge. They are thrillingly alert and alive but seemingly unafraid. Like all products of evolution, they are perfectly adapted to their environment, but the birds of the swamp share another characteristic that's a bonus to those who look at them: they are all shaped beautifully.

Red-shouldered hawks

119

Now I've seen the same birds—ibises, egrets, storks, anhingas, herons—in marshes and on beaches and in other swampy places and they're beautiful there, too. But in the deep, whispering wilderness of Okefenokee, where all the lines are dark green vertical or blackly horizontal, the curves of the ibises' beaks, the egrets' necks, the herons' wings, all these are gorgeous.

Everything else is impressively straight, but the roundness, the clear arcs of color make every view complicated and lovely.

Presumably because centuries of experience have proved it safest, most of the birds are high up most of the time. Their nests are in thick groves, well above the water and its predators. At rest, the birds grab branches with their huge feet and show their curves against the sky or the tapestry of waving Spanish moss.

Their shapes, their colors, their careless availability combine with the background to make it all perfectly photogenic.

Turkey vulture

I had one spring weekend free. Larry Calvert, the refuge manager at Okefenokee, knew a crowded rookery. So I met him early Saturday in a heavy Georgia rain.

The rookery occupied an entire "home." A home is what they call an island of trees and vines in the vast prairie, part land, mostly water, which is characteristic of the eastern part of the swamp.

At the very bottom of Okefenokee there is sand, covered by peat made of very old and dead vegetation.

Big chunks of peat break away once in a while, float to the surface and become a place for trees and bushes to grow. That happens often so the landscape moves and changes from year to year and there are homes of all ages, identifiable by the size of the trees, the thickness of the roots and brush.

White ibises—the darker birds are immature

Between the homes, there are acres of water lilies and reeds and heavy grasses. Trails are cut through the growth but near the homes, within a couple of hundred yards of them, the green is so thick and strong that no propeller can function. So we lifted up the motor and poled in closer.

It was hot and damp, the rain came and went away intermittently but the sky stayed gray. It was hard to work and the prospects for pictures were as dim as the misty yellow sun. But it was irresistible.

The home, no more than a quarter of a mile long and only half that wide, trembled with birds. They shrieked, croaked, cried, whimpered, fluttered, flew, fed, and posed. From one end of the island to the other, they had arranged their colonies into clearly marked territories. At the far left were white ibises, hundreds of them. Next to them, on the farther side of the home from where we stopped to look, there were cattle egrets, brilliantly white but streaked now with orange feathers of the breeding season. They overlapped into the domain of the bigger, whiter, more regal American egrets. Nearest us, noisiest, busiest, were the grandly purple little blue herons. And at the farthest right end, at higher levels and on branches farther out, were the anhingas, more often called snakebirds or water turkeys. Their bodies seem as pliable as snakes' and they wind their necks and wings into glorious black silhouettes.

As ever, I wanted to get closer. The water was warm and shallow and the peat bottom was smooth, Larry told me. He rejected my suggestion about taking off my boots. Too many snakes.

Out of the boat, ankle deep in grasping mud, sweating, trying to move, I was found by the mosquitoes. Their attacking fog of noise and pain drove me back, maddened and revolted.

Just a little oily repellent solved the infuriating problem and I waded back. Deep into the home.

I worked ineptly, clumsily. I discovered early that stopping caused my feet to sink deeply and, once, it took a major sweating effort to pull my foot and boot out of the bottom without losing either. I fell three times, was soaked to the neck, was cut on the forehead and back by branches, was truly lost, was sublimely happy.

Larry, cool and dry in his little boat, laughed a lot.

What I got were a hundred cuts and bites, a couple of dozen photographs, and the certain knowledge that I had been where I didn't belong. In the home, under a tattered canopy of leaves and gray sky, brown branches caked with white droppings, it was nearly silent. The wind caused twigs to creak and some of the tiny birds purred and murmured, but mostly I heard my own labored breath and ungainly splashing. So I stopped.

Egrets and ibises (opposite) and an immature white ibis

Thoreau had written the admonition: "You must walk so gently as to hear the finest sounds, the faculties being in repose. Your mind must not perspire."

I was in the center of someone else's world and my mind was not perspiring. I stood still for fifteen timed minutes, my feet on a submerged root, my head among five nests, three with pretty trios of light blue eggs, two with tiny panting birds. There were many small sounds, some bad odors, and many good ones. I saw many spectacular insects, very few adult birds, no snakes. It was dappled and patterned under the brush, damp and warm. It was a wonderfully foreign place.

American egret (left) and cattle egret

Cattle egret

Little blue herons

138

Louisiana heron and (opposite) white ibis and little blue heron

Anhingas

Apparently the big birds got used to me after a few minutes because they began to settle in although they stayed near the top of the umbrella above me. From below I watched a few territorial encounters, loud arguments among white ibises and cattle egrets. At my level, the baby birds were actively croaking, as though cheering for their parents. Actually, of course, they were marking their locations with the instinctive hope that they would be fed. Not while I was there, so I left.

Anhingas

Nestling cattle egrets

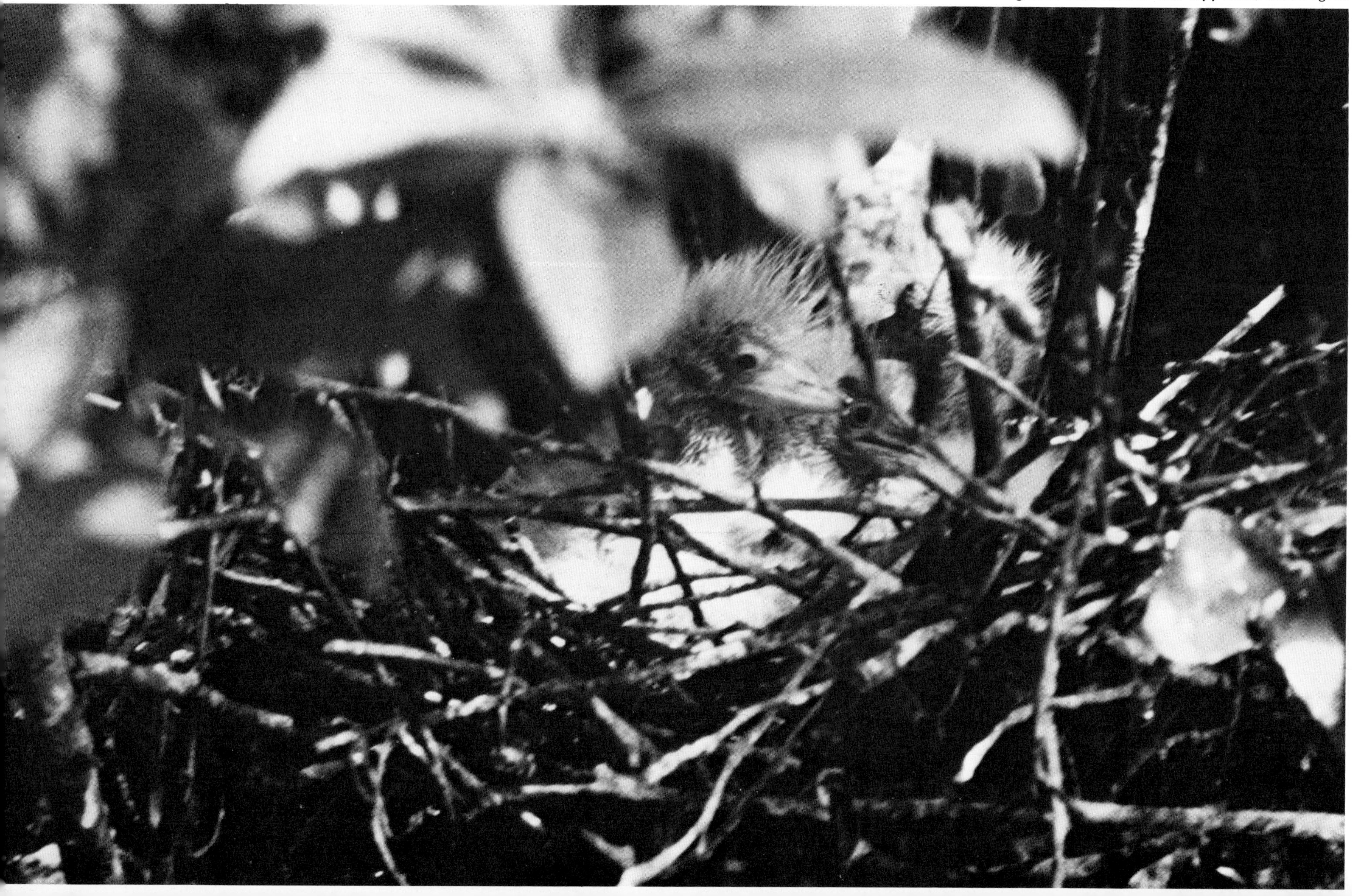

Nestling little blue herons and (opposite) cattle egret

Louisiana heron and (opposite) egrets, ibises and herons at home

Clean and dry, I went back to the home at sunset, this time in an airboat that took us right to the edge. We drifted silently for an hour while the egrets and ibises streaked in for roosting. They piled onto every branch of every tree and bush and the uncountable thousands of them were quiet before total darkness hid them.

They were home. ■

This chapter is a dirty trick. It's about a paradise for bird-watchers where almost no one is permitted to go. The Hawaiian Islands National Wildlife Refuge is off limits to just about everyone and that's the only reason it exists.

Once it had been an Eden. Then men came to it and it became a kind of Hell. Now, isolated and guarded and patrolled, it is virtually uninhabited. It is grand and gorgeous, a paradise restored.

The refuge is a slim arc of minute atolls, called the Leeward Islands, that swing out northwest from the main Hawaiian group. It is well over 99 per cent water. But on each of the 1,765 acres of rock and coral in the immense ocean—on them, in them, over and around them—there are millions and millions of birds.

The water is brilliant and warm and it teems with food for hordes of soaring birds, which find their way ashore very seldom, and then only to mate and nest. Most of them do everything else—mostly eating—out at sea. There is almost nothing to eat on the tiny bits of land.

What there is on those dozen or so islets, surely the most remote bits of American landscape, is an unsurpassed experience. Because there are so many unafraid birds, it is possible to stay and move among them and learn something of what it must be to be a bird.

I was there one winter week with a film crew to do a couple of television stories. We lived on one of the islands, the only one with people on it. French Frigate Shoals is 3,000 yards long and 300 wide; it has an airstrip and several things they call trees. The eighteen Coast Guardsmen who operate the navigation station there are outnumbered about a hundred-to-one by Laysan albatrosses, "gooney birds."

For the first four days of our visit, we watched gooneys, old movies, each other, torrential rain, and the barometer. None of these offered any encouragement. On the fifth day (our escape airplane was coming on the sixth) the barometer zoomed up, the sun scorched the sky and water and we regained our ability to smile. In motor boats, we darted to sandy islands a few miles away and entered paradise.

More than a mile from shore, the frigatebirds came to assemble around us. We had watched them hover high in the immaculate sky, but as we got closer to their island, they dropped close.

Close means five to ten feet. The frigatebird has a wingspan of about seven feet, a very long, hooked beak, and a terrible reputation as a pirate and tyrant. They are so big and they were so close and so many that their threatening shadows put us in the cool dark. I reached up to the closest one, touched his black belly and caused him to drift up about ten feet without a sound or any apparent effort. Eerily, the sun burst through the new hole in the shadow mass. With a few minute manipulations of their forked tails and pointed wing tips, the frigates rose to join a huge, squawking flock of sooty terns floating much higher above the island.

We landed and did our movie-making in a little over two hours. That left about six hours to explore and feel. I went off by myself to photograph and let this wonderful place engulf me. In my camera bag, I had an old book that helped explain the wonder.

It told of how things were on these islands until the first decade of the twentieth century. At that time, outlandish plumes for women's hats were popular. So an entrepreneur recruited a band of Japanese workers, came to the Leewards, and began harvesting whole wings. In 1903, a naturalist named William A. Bryan came to the islands and wrote glowing descriptions of this "bird Heaven."

He made another visit in 1911. By then, the bird hunters had come and killed and been driven out by the federal government. (The atolls had been made a National Refuge in 1909.) This is a part of his description of Laysan, the biggest of the islets, after just eight years of hunting:

The slaughter wrought by the plume hunters is everywhere apparent. One of the work buildings used . . . as a storehouse by the poachers is still standing. With a side torn out and left open to the weather, it is still filled with thousands of pairs of albatross wings. Though weather-beaten and useless, they show how they were cut from the birds whose half-bleached skeletons lie in thousands of heaps scattered all over the island.

Blue-faced boobies (foreground) and black-footed albatrosses

This wholesale killing has had an appalling effect on this colony. No one can estimate the thousands, perhaps hundreds of thousands, of birds that have been willfully sacrificed on Laysan to the whim of fashion and the lust of gain. It is conservative to say that fully one-half the number of birds of both species of albatross that were so abundant everywhere in 1903 have been killed. The colonies that remain are in a sadly decimated condition. Often a colony of a dozen or more birds will not have a single young.

Over a large part of the island, in some sections a hundred acres in a place, that 10 years ago was thickly inhabited by albatrosses, not a single bird remains, while heaps of the slain lie as mute testimony of the awful slaughter of these beautiful, harmless, and without doubt beneficial inhabitants of the high seas.

But Mr. Bryan was also a prophet:

Fortunately, serious as were the depredations of the poachers, their operations were interrupted before any of the species had been completely exterminated. So far as the birds that secure their food from the sea are concerned, it is reasonable to suppose they will increase in number, and that nature will in time restore the island to its former populous condition if no further slaughter is permitted.

Well, none is. Not only no slaughter but no visiting, no importing of new mammals or birds or weeds or seeds. To get ashore, you need a federal permit and a fairly good reason for getting one. All this stringency has done nothing less than recreate Mr. Bryan's "bird Heaven."

Brown booby

This is how it was on one of the islands for part of just one day:

Near the shore, on the sloping edge of the island, there were blue-faced boobies. They are big white birds with long yellow bills. Their close relatives, the red-faced boobies, have blue bills. (To confuse the identifier further, there is a dark brown booby named the brown booby.)

Blue-faced boobies

The nest of the blue-faced is that place in the sand where the eggs happen to be; there is no other means of specifying it among the other thousands of square feet of sand. The red-footed has a more traditional nest of twigs in the low shrub. Clearly, the two species have separate territories but, to my delight, they share the habit of fearlessness. It was possible to walk to within four or five feet of either of them without causing alarm. Getting closer caused them to scream away but neither of them used its tremendous bill against me.

Mostly I squatted and looked at them. They looked back with no indication of alarm or wonderment or even interest. It was very pleasant, if not flattering.

Red-footed boobies

159

Red-footed boobies and Hawaiian monk seal

Black-footed albatross

The island is about a mile long, a quarter mile wide and almost perfectly flat. The highest point is a towering ten feet above sea level. After a very short time spent exploring, it became evident to me that the place is carefully zoned.

At the edges, in and just beyond the surf, the rare Hawaiian monk seals haul ashore. There are fewer than 2,000 of them in the world and we saw an impressive percentage—more than 50—on that single afternoon. Most were big gray cows with small, black, bleating pups. The cows are aggressively protective and thrash about heavily but quickly when an intruder gets close. They roar hoarsely and show a lot of teeth. For me, their most effective weapon was almost unbelievably bad breath. The smell of a decade of digested squid and fish drove me back in tears.

The boobies form a ring all around the island. The blue-faced on the sand, the red-footed in the few heavy shrubs. Inside those are quite distinct colonies of the two albatrosses, black-footed (which are dark gray) and Laysan (which are mostly white). Both are called gooneys.

Black-footed albatrosses

Black-footed albatrosses and (opposite) Laysan albatrosses

Laysan albatrosses

At just about the middle of the atoll, in the only patch of scrub, the great frigatebirds nest (that's their official name and differentiates them from magnificent frigatebirds, also official). Beyond them, on the open sand, is the immense colony of sooty terns. They're called sooty because they have dark backs and heads but my first sight of them made me think they were pure white. I saw them from below while they wheeled and hovered very high in the piercingly blue sky.

And there were territories up there, too. The terns, masses of them, were highest. The boobies flew back and forth between land and sea at medium altitude. The gooneys took off slow and low until they cleared the whole pattern of other birds and then soared up. Patrolling in a large group and at all altitudes were the frigates. They rose and dropped, soared a little way off shore, floated back over their nests, apparently moving with no effort but with obvious alertness and careful plan.

The frigates got their name (and their other name, man-o'-war bird) from their technique of piratical feeding. I watched a half-dozen separate forays in which a frigate pounced on a booby in mid-air and grabbed a dropped chunk of food intended for some young booby on the sand. The frigates ganged up on the smaller bird but never seemed to fight over the disgorged prize. In each instance, the booby wheeled back out to sea and more food.

On that day, at that island, the frigates were in the nesting season. Many females were half-buried on their nests in the green bushes. The immatures, just as big but marked by light-colored heads, were flying in a large flock. In a separate flock, a smaller one, were the spectacular breeding males. Their huge, scarlet gular pouches were fully inflated and made a fantasy of the air: very white clouds, intensely blue sky, big black birds with great patches of the brightest red at their throats.

A few of the males were on their nests, clacking their bills, fussily moving twigs, flashing their bizarre red pouches while a few unmated females looked around from overhead.

Obviously it works. There are lots of new frigate-birds hatched each year.

At the edge of the man-o'-war real estate there was a shrub with a nest holding a red-footed booby on it. I moved close in to photograph the booby. Too close—she flew away. Immediately, an immature frigatebird settled into the brush and ignored me utterly, even when I moved within five feet. Repeatedly, the booby flapped back to the nest, settled for a moment and squawked away again. I watched until finally the frigate clumsily hopped onto the nest. The booby gave up and flew away.

The frigatebird had no need for a nest; it was sexually immature. But if there were booby eggs, they would soon be eaten. My intrusion had scared away the protector.

It was a small and classic case of ecological blunder. With such good motives and such open hearts and minds, we go where we don't belong without knowing anything about what we're doing. It was a terrifying microcosm and my confession doesn't make me feel any better—only smarter.

Most of the time I watched albatrosses struggling to get aloft, soaring, waddling, puffing and dancing, squatting in awkward parenthood right on top of a tiny chick, staring but mostly courting. Gooneys are famous (with those who know of their existence at all) for two things: their absolute territorial fidelity, which makes them virtually immovable, and their antic courtship dances, which make them fascinating.

The first quality caused the U.S. Navy tremendous trouble. The birds' faithfulness to their nesting sites resulted in thousands of airplane accidents on and above those Pacific islands where both airplanes and gooneys exist. Everything from terrain reconstruction to genocide has been tried but there are still gooneys in large numbers and collisions in slightly smaller ones.

At the time an albatross is old enough to leave its nest permanently, it goes out to sea for a full two years. Then it returns to the place where it was hatched—the exact place. Numerous studies of banded birds have shown that they come back to within a yard of the spot where they had hacked their way out of the egg! Another test involved releasing two captive birds in the State of Washington. They reappeared at their nests on Midway Island ten days later—3,200 miles away. They must have found westbound currents and soared home, almost never stopping to rest or eat.

Such commitment is a powerful survival factor. So is the mad courtship behavior. Fortunately for bird-watchers, the gooneys keep up their dancing long after mating and nesting has been finished.

I watched for hours on that sandy suburb of French Frigate Shoals. I watched and photographed and gave up trying to understand the ritual. From time to time, I referred to my old book. In it is a description written by an observer of the rite nearly seventy years ago. Nothing has changed since:

This game or whatever one may wish to call it, very likely originated in past time during the courting season, but it certainly has long since lost any such significance. At first two birds approach one another, bowing profoundly and stepping heavily. They swagger about each other, nodding and courtseying solemnly, then suddenly begin to fence a little, crossing bills and whetting them together, sometimes with a whistling sound, meanwhile pecking and dropping stiff little bows. All at once one lifts its closed wing and nibbles at the feathers beneath, or rarely, if in a hurry, quickly turns its head. The partner during this short performance assumes a statuesque pose and either looks mechanically from side to side or snaps its bill loudly a few times. Then the first bird bows once, and pointing its head and beak straight upward, rises on its toes, puffs out its breast and utters a prolonged, nasal, "ah-h-h-," with a rapidly rising inflection and with a distinctly "anserine" and "bovine" quality, quite difficult to describe. While this "song" is being uttered the companion loudly and rapidly snaps its bill. Often both birds raise their heads in air and either one or both favor the appreciative audience with that ridiculous and indescribable bovine groan. When they have finished they begin bowing to each other again, rapidly and alternately, and presently repeat the performance, the birds reversing their role in the game or not. In the most successful dances the movements are executed in perfect unison and this fact much enhances the extraordinary effect.

Laysan albatrosses

Laysan and (opposite) black-footed albatrosses

There were thousands of pairs of gooneys and both the black-footed and Laysan birds gave their performances repeatedly. A more thorough student could tell the differences between the dances of the two species. They were identically entrancing to me.

After several hours and many rolls of film, I became aware that I had been alone and busy with the birds for a long time. I was at home there, relaxed and comfortable. My perceptions were acute, the experience was intense, I was very involved in everything going on around me, in tune with all the movement and color and sound. That's how a bird lives —a fantastic metabolic rate, very high blood temperature, much movement and response, acute senses, little sleep. I was remarkably close to being what these beautiful things are. The relationship seemed to be one of total intimacy.

It was wonderful and I was free.

But it wasn't intimacy. Real intimacy, I know, involves some kind of love, and the birds, for all their acceptance and courage and beauty and unfettered spirits, gave me none of that. And intimacy involves communication. I have learned much about birds and freedom and exhilaration from that day and many like it. From all of that, I have come to believe that whatever I had with them (and still have in other places, at many times), it is not intimacy. We didn't communicate.

The beautiful, beautiful birds enchant me and I need them. But more, I need connection. The fact that they don't is a part of appreciating them and of understanding us. ■

Fairy terns

My living room is high so my Christmas tree is tall and heavy. Once it was terribly destructive. It crashed down and flung me off a ladder where I was busy tying it up so that just that thing wouldn't happen. My failure sprained my ankle.

I drooped around on crutches for weeks, nearly helpless, crippled by disappointment and pain. It hurt all the time. It burned, it ached, it irritated. That was the pain.

The disappointment was this: it had taken massive manipulation to arrange an assignment to produce a television program in Dallas in late January. That was to bring me near Muleshoe, Texas, the same place and same time that Muleshoe acquires its very limited fame as the meeting place of an apparently limitless flock of sandhill cranes. Every year the huge birds winter on this speck of a refuge, more of them each year, so many of them that conservationists have decided that there are now enough of them to be hunted as they were just before they became too few.

Once they had been plentiful. But they are remarkably edible and hunters are hungry. So they got shot and they got rare and then protected. Now, again, they are many.

Sandhill cranes are among the tallest American birds —almost five feet tall and straight, usually called stately, proud. They are several shades of gray simultaneously except for the tops of their heads, which are red. They're the ones who do the dramatic nuptial dances. That results in more sandhill cranes and, for me, a challenge.

In Florida, Georgia, Utah, Oregon, Louisiana— everywhere I asked—men told me how plentiful they are. Finally, after knowing sandhill cranes from dozens of bird books and dozens of stories, I saw a pair in northern California. They were wildly wonderful, dancing and growling, leaping and fluttering strongly, tantalizing me to meet them in numbers at a frozen Texas prairie.

I had the date and no ankle agony could keep me from them. A postponement would have been, unspeakably, for a year.

I tried it with a cane instead of crutches. The pain was as severe and as constant, but I now could hope to carry my sixty pounds of camera gear onto the plane to Lubbock. A rented car with a radio that obviously was tuned only for Spanish country music carried me over a path of ice marked U.S. 84. It hurt to accelerate, it hurt to brake, it hurt to just sit with the ankle against the heater. Sometimes it all seemed very foolish.

In Muleshoe, a call to the refuge manager did nothing for my pained spirits. Mr. Hansen was expecting me <u>next</u> weekend and this was a very bad time. But, like his colleagues on all the National Wildlife Refuges, Mr. Hansen has compassion for those travelers, swathed in inappropriate clothing and long lenses, who come to see the birds. He invited me out to his place in the late, gelid afternoon.

I stopped to buy the essentials I lacked: thermal long underwear, a hat with warm earflaps, a rather vast quantity of Jack Daniel's.

In the twenty miles of driving from Muleshoe to the refuge, I saw two other cars, at least a dozen coveys of scaled quail, and hundreds of sandhill cranes: at all altitudes, on every possible heading, they flapped and squawked in long lines toward the same goal as I. It took me well over an hour to make the drive because I stopped frequently to marvel at the birds. I leaned on my cane, and I would like to say I remembered what Homer had written, what Thoreau had quoted. I remembered only the two authors' names; I looked it up much later:

... advanced as a flight of cranes that scream overhead when rain and winter drive them over the flowing waters of Oceanus to bring death and destruction on the pygmies, and they wrangle in the air as they fly.

Their mission, of course, was far more benign and less romantic. The cranes and I were headed for a place to rest and commune. And while we made our way there, most of the daylight got away from us.

Out of the dusk the birds swooped onto the little lakes of the refuge. Mr. Hansen showed me how the greatest number were headed over the near hills to Paul's Lake beyond. They would be there, thousands of them, in the icy dawn, and he suggested that I get some rest before then. I was to go alone and he showed me how to unlock the gate and drive near the lake. He lent me the key, wished me luck, and invited me to come back some time tomorrow.

I spent the night in a motel, soaking and re-taping my ankle, eating some sandwiches, drinking some whisky and watching—so help me!—a rerun of The Birds on television. I got up at four, dressed extravagantly, had a pre-dawn breakfast in a diner where a waitress, a janitor, and I discoursed freely and favorably on the work of Alfred Hitchcock, and went to the pond.

It was 13 above zero, the wind was gusting to 45 miles an hour and there were frequent snow squalls. It was very dark.

From the securely locked gate to the place the dirt road cuts closest to the lake is a couple of miles. It's another mile, down a gentle slope of rocks and frozen mud, to the place where a 1,000-mm. lens pulls the cranes close enough to be photographed. I limped and slid that last mile toward the barely visible pond, which seemed to be covered by gray lumpy ice.

The gray lumps, I finally learned, were more than 50,000 sandhill cranes. They were packed into the unfrozen center of Paul's Lake and the same color as the water, the ice, the weeds, the hills, the sky. Only their shapes and their movements and their increasing noisiness etched them away from their environment.

When I got halfway to the shoreline, they began taking off. Large flocks (150 or so), small flocks (about twenty birds), or pairs, and even individuals would spring up screaming. They circled and searched and most flew off. Some settled back. But all the movement ... and several thousand must have flown away in the half hour before dawn became official ... all the motion seemed to diminish the standing flock not at all.

The light was dim and it was terribly, terribly cold. I was alone and my ankle hurt very much.

I was in the midst of a spectacle but I was helpless. Photographing was a waste of time and film. The humidity caused my breath to frost every part of the camera it touched. I was as close to the cranes as I could get and, when I could see through the ice-covered view finder, there wasn't much to see. I shot some pictures, listlessly, because I have learned that there are darkroom miracles beyond my comprehension. The motor on the camera was frozen, so sequences of flight photographs were impossible. My disappointment was about complete.

After ninety minutes, encumbered by my heavy clothing and my heavy gear, and spiritless, cold, and hurting, I started up the slope toward the scarlet Chevrolet on the horizon. In the 360 degrees of gray, it was a spot of mocking color.

I stopped frequently to rest. After a half-hour, I had gone less than a quarter of a mile directly into the battering wind. My dragging boot suddenly caught in a hole and I fell. The pain was awful.

I was unable to stand on that leg. After trying, I suppose I fell again. I assume I remained conscious because now, years later, I still can recreate the fear, which was worst when I was blinded by tears that froze my eyes shut.

I tried any number of stupid things. Probably the most bizarre was removing my boot and sock and tape and warming my offending ankle with a blazing Zippo lighter. The wind ate up the fuel quickly and nothing came of that.

Incredibly, I probably would have died there if I hadn't moved.

(The squalls increased to a blizzard and, later, an ice storm through the day; the temperature didn't get above 20. Mr. Hansen told me later he would not have thought to go looking for me before evening; no one else could because the distant gate was locked.)

How to move was a question to be pondered in what had become a dangerously sleepy state.

I could drag all the equipment up to the car, I could drag some to the car and get warm and come back for the rest, I could abandon it and get myself to the car and hope to find the valuable stuff in the snow some time later. While I pondered, the cranes suddenly began taking off in larger numbers.

So I stopped pondering and began taking pictures. It took great effort and much time just to set up the machinery. Then, lying on my back, the tripod straddling me, the long lens pointed straight up, I finished a roll of partly exposed film. To reload was impossible.

I capped the lens, folded up the equipment, and slowly crawled with it, happily, to the car.

It is not possible for me to trace out the source of my determination or to evaluate the symbols or meaning of my long crawl. I know that I had a different attitude about getting to the car after I took those few pictures. I know, too, that I cherish the experience for no reason other than that it was flagrantly unique. I know that one of those pictures is my favorite from among many hundreds.

I know that, in that picture, is all the reason why I went to the pond.

And why I came back.

This, from <u>Walden</u>:

I went to the pond because I wished to live deliberately, to front only the essential facts of life, and see if I could not learn what it had to teach, and not, when I came to die, discover that I had not lived. I did not wish to live what was not life, living is so dear; nor did I wish to practice resignation, unless it was quite necessary. . . . ∎

In 1964, to celebrate absolutely nothing, I sought out a spectacle. I found it at Bonaventure Island, a spot a mile off the Gaspé Peninsula in the Gulf of St. Lawrence. There are murres there and gulls and auks and a half-dozen human families and more than 10,000 breeding, nesting, soaring, screaming, gleaming white gannets.

Any gannet is big—almost three feet long with a six foot wingspan—but this island of them is a seething enormity. In midsummer it looks like an Alpine meadow in midwinter, a white plateau hovering above the blue ocean.

The gannetry is the eastern edge of Bonaventure. Between it and the western side, where there are cabins and a few farmhouses, there is a silent evergreen forest. Where the birds are is noisily alive. The gannets cover every square foot of open land, much of the air and great parts of the sea.

To walk to them is a doubtful trip. The slippery path through the foggy woods gives no hint of the openness and liveliness of the bird cliffs. But where the forest ends the nesting ground begins. The sky, the shrieks, the rush of beauty hits suddenly, memorably.

John James Audubon, a man accustomed to witnessing spectacles, reacted this way when he first saw a gannet colony in 1833:

I could distinguish [the rock] plainly from the deck, and thought it covered with snow to the depth of several feet; this appearance existed on every portion of the flat, projecting shelves. . . . I rubbed my eyes, took my spyglass and in an instant the strangest picture stood before me. They were birds we saw—a mass of birds of such a size I never before cast my eyes on. . . . The nearer we approached the greater our surprise at the enormous number of these birds, all calmly seated on their eggs or newly hatched brood, their heads all turned to windward and toward us. The air above for a hundred yards, and for some distance around the whole rock, was filled with gannets on the wing, which, from our position, made it appear as if a heavy fall of snow was directly above us.

There are far fewer gannets now than there were when Audubon sailed the Gulf. They were nearly wiped out by bird hunters. But they're coming back in what are now Canadian National Refuges. All along the edge of the Bonaventure colony there are signs, in English and French, warning: "No Hunting! No Egging!"

There are, of course, no unnatural restrictions on viewing or listening or taking pictures. There are even some crude platforms jutting over the cliff edge. You can walk out onto very thin air and look straight down at thousands of birds and rocks and hammering surf, if rain or fog or acrophobia don't get in the way. On my visit, I was accompanied (and pushed) by my son and his typically fifteen-year-old sense of adventure.

Repeatedly we hiked through the woods, hung over the lip of the cliff, and stared and listened. Frequently, we lay on our backs at the edge of the colony and followed individual gannets as they maneuvered through the clouds of birds, peering down, treading air.

Joe scouted busily. He kept finding niches and little draws where I could stretch out and hang over and shoot down. Strongly, he held me by my belt or my ankles. He knew no fear and I knew little else. The red sandstone wall, washed by rough winds, is just about vertical—twenty stories high. But from the gannet-covered top to the surf, the wall is dramatically etched by bird-bearing ledges. Kittiwakes crowd with their backs to the sea, murres and razorbills face out. Obviously, it was worth the risk to get some pictures.

We were there for four days. Every foggy morning we went across the island, waited for clear skies, shot every picture we could think of and returned to the auberge for a tremendous event of Gaspesian haute cuisine. But in the afternoon, we'd always decide to trek through the forest to the gannets again. After a day and a half of hardy hiking, Joe made a deal. He found a young driver and an ancient wooden wagon with a horse of matching age and condition. In his incredibly broken French, Joe convinced the idle teamster that a round trip to the gannetry for us and a near-ton of camera gear was worth about a dollar. We traveled comfortably from then on.

We lived happily with an open fire on the freezing nights, with many handmade quilts on wooden beds without mattresses, with much fog and more sunshine and with beautiful birds. For many hours, we watched how the buff color of the gannets' heads changed as they turned in the sun, how the birds hovered to find their chicks in the mob of identical others, how they soared past and turned their heads sidelong to stare at us, how their flight changed from a soar to a hover to a plummet as they swooped deep for fish, how they never panicked but almost never stopped humming or crying or squawking. We both remember the sounds and smells but remember best a single, repeated sight: how the blue of the bird's huge eye matched precisely the sky where he was home.

Something else wonderful happened to us at Bonaventure. Two lady schoolteacher bird-watchers told us how, by detouring slightly on the way home, we could get to a place where we could photograph puffins. We had seen puffins stuffed in museums and pictured in books, but always assumed they were some kind of Arctic oceanic myth. Supposedly they exist on Bonaventure; surely they do on Machias Seal Island. The nice ladies had seen them there a week earlier.

The island technically is part of the United States, but there has been some doubt about that in the past so Canada maintains the lighthouse there, as it has for a long time. It doesn't matter much except that if it's in Maine, it's one of just two places on the U.S. East Coast where puffins nest. If it's Canadian, it's one of several.

Captain Purcell Corbett of Cutler took us out to the island. It's about fifteen miles from shore. If you go, you can expect a smooth-running boat, a very friendly Down East captain, a superb fish chowder cooked aboard, and no wasted conversation.

The captain knows his puffins (and his rocks, tides, shoals, boat, coastline, weather, and sky) but sees no need to talk much. He is a private man, a New Englander. He is strong and smart and he took me where I thought I'd never go.

A mile or so from Machias Seal, Captain Corbett pointed astern. "They-ah!" he shouted. It was our first puffin, tiny, beating quickly through the wind to the island. We chugged in along the shore and the captain pointed up to the tops of the rocks. Not even one word this time. But forty puffins lined up looking out. I know the number because I took a picture and I've counted them a hundred times since.

There really isn't much to say about puffins beyond what a photograph of just one says better. They are hilarious, unlikely, charming, enchanting. Even seeing them does not dismiss their unbelievability. The people who run the lighthouse at Machias Seal think they are wonderful and they like the puffin-watchers, too. So they've built some small blinds in the nesting area and we were able to spend a long day laughing while we watched.

The nestling birds are deep in burrows and completely hidden. They moan incessantly. The parent birds flutter out to sea for a beakful of small fish many times a day. From the blind, we could spot the burrows only by watching where the puffins walked out of sight. Puffins are pretty good flyers, and apparently good underwater swimmers, but ridiculous walkers. They step gingerly on the tips of their toes and waddle around the rocks. They do a great deal of bowing and rubbing beaks with their mates and growl a little, all with a very silly quizzical expression caused by the upturned lines above their eyes.

It is impossible for me to watch them without smiling and without forgetting that they are birds. They really seem and behave like prissy little men, very busy and very charming.

Their charm has attracted me to puffinries around half the world. Once to the British Isles, where there are many of them. There is even an island there, Lundy, that coins its own money in two denominations: a puffin and a half-puffin. There is another island, Skomer, off the coast of Wales, that has no coins but lots of birds, bluebells, and a single tree.

Atlantic puffins

Atlantic puffin with a half dozen fish (opposite) and forty more puffins

There I went one time with my wife for an overnight stay. We were almost alone on the 740 acres of grass and wild flowers, alone except for thousands and thousands of birds. Hundreds of them were puffins. For two days, we were soaked by the dew and fog and amused by the "sea parrots" who are just as comic there. We watched them swoop around the rocks, huddle together, waddle aimlessly, and crash into the ocean. Often, they looked at us head-on and shrugged and looked away.

The island is empty of people except for the warden and his family and, in the warm months, daily visitors who come to see razorbills, kittiwakes, oystercatchers, murres, and puffins. Puffins in Wales are essentially no different from those in Maine: all of them are comedians.

Another time and in another faraway place, I sprawled again in wet grass, in high wind, to look over a cliff edge to watch the little comedians. In the Pribilof Islands, in the Bering Sea off Alaska, near Siberia, there are two different kinds of puffins. One, called horned, is about like those in the Atlantic except that it has a little protrusion sticking up above each eye. The other, the tufted puffin, is quite different, maybe even more bizarre. It's almost all black, its bill is longer and differently colored, although again bright orange and yellow and white, and it has sweeping golden plumes arching back from above its eyes.

I've gone back again to Machias Seal with Captain Corbett, too. It was too late, really, and most of the puffins had flown out to sea for the winter. It was too rough to get ashore so we just got seasick. No puffins, no pictures and, please, no fish chowder.

I have gone far just to see puffins. Always they were on islands where there were very few people but many other birds. There was cold wind and roaring, driving surf. In each of those places there is magnificent aloneness and sounds of free wind, screaming gulls, heavy rain on thick tangled grass. Puffins live where the air is immaculate.

But I'll go again to see puffins just because I like to look at them. Not because they represent anything as lofty and desirable as freedom or because they symbolize what I seek. I just like to look at them because they are funny little people.

Now anthropomorphism, the attribution to other animals of those qualities which are essentially men's, is some kind of crime to scientists. Birds are birds and bugs are bugs and people are people and it's wrong to see ourselves in them. I know and accept it but, in the case of these birds, I ignore it.

For these curious, waddling, all-dressed-up, bowing and moaning little showmen with their false noses and painted cheeks are clowns. Of course they don't mean to be. I know they have the very dimmest awareness of me and that I relate little to their experience.

But they relate to mine and that makes it fun. Anthropomorphism is fun. Eagles are enjoyable because they represent something nobly human, owls are appreciated as symbols of wisdom because they look something like what we think wise men look like, sandpipers are amusing because they appear to be dainty and polite when they eat the way we want our children to eat. Looking at birds as people is harmless. It's fun. That's what bird-watching should be. ■

Tufted puffin diving

There are two blinds on Machias Seal island. This is the view of one from the other. People inside probably wonder where all the puffins went.

Horned puffins

Horned puffin (opposite) and European puffins

European puffins and (opposite) horned puffins

About twenty years ago, when I was a young newspaper reporter in Chicago, I covered an uncharacteristic Chicago story. It was a press conference at the imposing Encyclopaedia Britannica offices to announce and describe the publication of <u>The Great Books of the Western World</u>. The event, like the books, was fancy and impressive and expensive.

Most of the questions from the scruffy reporters to the overbearing eggheads (a contemporary term applied to anyone who appeared better-educated or less-menially employed) concerned the price of the books.

But some asked why their favorites were not included in the fifty or so volumes that ranged, chronologically, from Homer to Freud. After considerable snobbish anti-snob questioning and considerable pedantic defense, someone asked, remarkably, why the Bible was not included.

"The Bible," answered Dr. Mortimer J. Adler, "is assumed."

That's how it is with <u>Walden</u> and me. I don't just read it, carry it with me, study it, think about it, depend on it. I assume it.

I've read <u>Walden</u> and books about <u>Walden</u> and books about books about <u>Walden</u>. I've discovered new meanings in it frequently. Strangely, I've memorized very little of it.

I don't think I know nearly as much about its author from all the reading of it as I do about the reader. I have found it to be a guidebook, an atlas to be used in travels along unmarked trails. It's a series of angry injunctions and imperatives that help me.

Most practically, <u>Walden</u> provides the ideas for my photographs.

Right near the beginning of <u>Walden</u>, in the second paragraph, the distinguished author wrote:

In most books, the "I," or first person, is omitted; in this it will be retained; that, in respect to egotism, is the main difference. We commonly do not remember that it is, after all, always the first person that is speaking. I should not talk so much about myself if there were any body else whom I knew as well. Unfortunately, I am confined to this theme by the narrowness of my experience. Moreover, I, on my side, require of every writer, first or last, a simple and sincere account of his own life, and not merely what he has heard of other men's lives; some such account as he would send to his kindred from a distant land; for if he has lived sincerely, it must have been in a distant land to me. Perhaps these pages are more particularly addressed to poor students. As for the rest of my readers, they will accept such portions as apply to them. I trust that none will stretch the seams in putting on the coat, for it may do good service to him whom it fits.

Thoreau then went on to write a classic so rich in "I's" that the typesetters ran out of them from time to time.

Avocet (opposite) and immature roseate spoonbills

I propose herewith to adopt the defiant Thoreau apologia for myself. This chapter is one long "I" in picture form, a pictorial statement of what I think beauty is and what I think is universally important. What follows is a group of pictures selected by me from among several thousand made by me under compulsion from no one but me. They are "a simple and sincere account of [my] own life . . ." that I hope will have some pertinence for readers and that "they will accept such portions as apply to them."

The pictures were made in many different places, over more than ten years. They have no connecting theme, nothing in common except this: all of them are glimpses of life, each was made by a happy photographer.■

Avocet

225

Louisiana herons and (opposite) avocets, various sandpipers and ring-billed gulls

Roseate spoonbill (opposite) and double-crested cormorant

Canada geese and (opposite) double-crested cormorants and herring gulls

Kittiwakes (left) and black skimmers

Canada geese and (opposite) roseate spoonbill

Roseate tern incubating a seashell and
(right) barn swallows feeding in my garage

Roseate spoonbill

Roseate spoonbill and (opposite) Canada geese

Snowy egrets and (opposite) semipalmated plovers

Black-bellied plovers (opposite) and American egret

Semipalmated plovers, I think

Avocets

Ducks (mallards, gadwalls, pintails, teal and widgeons) and (opposite) two-week-old roseate spoonbill

Sanderlings and (opposite) great blue herons

Black skimmers and (opposite) a snowy egret, dowitchers and sanderlings

Pintails

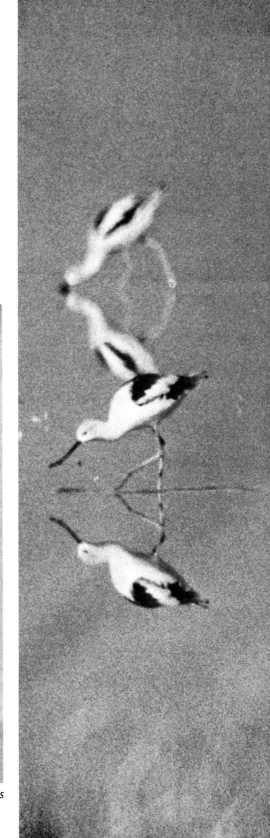

255

Avocets

Black skimmers and (opposite) Canada geese

White pelicans and (opposite) Canada geese

Canada geese

Snow geese (opposite) and Canadas

We used to call it "The Breakfast of Champions." Not Wheaties but calvados, which was sold to us by friendly French apple farmers in 1944 for a half a franc a bottle. It was brand-new, still smoking and sweating a little when we drank it to start another bad day.

Now it's very expensive and aged and smooth. But it's still a very effective starter on cold wet mornings when the fog hides your quarry and mysterious sounds divert you from the seeking. So there was a fancy little flask of calvados in my pocket as I started my third consecutive day of hunting for sandhill cranes in Okefenokee.

I already had that single good and memorable picture of them from Muleshoe. And a few from Klamath. But the cranes truly had outwitted me for years by being huge and available and loud-calling and wide-ranging and virtually unphotographable. It had always been because of the weather or a sore ankle or poor reflexes or tired eyes, but I missed hundreds of them. And for two precious days in the big Georgia swamp, even with expert guides, I missed a hundred more.

One of the days it rained and was cold. We saw cranes and I even made some dripping pictures of them fleeing from us. But we were drenched and very cold and without calvados so it was another failure in my mildly obsessive campaign for an uncommon picture of some rather common birds.

Next day was warm and beautifully sunny and I was captivated again by the green and gray and tan and black wilderness of Okefenokee. There were alligators and a few birds but just two of the reported 500 sandhills. I caught the familiar sight of their tail ends and had the usual disappointment of only views of their long legs dragging behind them, pointed straight at my lens.

So it was the third (and last) day of this vacation.

Larry Calvert, the refuge manager, had urged my visit because there were so few tourists and so many cranes. I saw neither for a long time that morning because all of Georgia and Florida were grayed by fog. No planes were flying, few cars were moving, and Okefenokee was a spooky sanctuary full of croaking, crying, quacking creatures hiding from me. Larry wisely found something to keep him busy indoors so I hit the swamp with Neb Bowen, another of those refuge people incapable of getting lost or irritable or defeated. He knew we'd find cranes and we wouldn't need sunshine, either.

It was incredibly foggy. We moved very slowly in the air boat, feeling suspended in the heavy cloud, lost from the sky and from the water. Everything was the same indistinct color and the shapes swirled and changed constantly. I saw no ducks, egrets, herons, anhingas, vultures, ibises, or alligators. And, of course, no sandhill cranes. But we heard all kinds of mocking things and we saw a lightness on part of the gray overhead that must have been the sun.

It was. Suddenly, it burned off the top half of the hemisphere above us. It was a brilliant and hot-looking blue from about twenty feet up to infinity. All around us, though, it was gray-green and damply lovely. It was possible to see the tops of trees clearly but they seemed to be growing out of a cloudy ground. We drifted into a field of these trunkless cypresses and it was alarming.

At the top of each and partway down from the top, too, there were immense birds with their wings spread for flight but not moving. There were more than a hundred of them and it was like being in a forest of totem poles.

Neb knew the place well. It was the roosting place for most of the swamp's turkey vultures—buzzards. They were drying their fog-soaked wings so they could soar and hunt. We waited and watched.

Turkey vultures

The sun dispersed the rest of the fog rather quickly.
Very soon, the swamp looked familiar again and the sky
was pure and washed. I made some pictures, sipped
some breakfast, and delightedly learned that Neb didn't
drink. We moved out after cranes.

Sandhill cranes

It can be told succinctly: we spent six more hours in the warm, sunny swamp, we saw at least 150 sandhill cranes, we finally learned that stopping the motor and drifting sometimes allows the cranes to circle back to where we flushed them. I made a great many pictures and some are satisfactory. But most of them are of tails and trailing legs.

My flask was empty. Sandhill cranes are champions. They still elude me.

They still beckon. ■

& The drive from San Francisco to Portland takes about thirteen hours but, if you work it right, it can take six days. Between the two cities, there are hundreds of miles of detours that connect islands of beauty unduplicated anywhere. I had traveled there several times so once I took my youngest son, Sam, to show him the wonders of the place. It developed that we showed it to each other.

We went there with a strong commitment to relax and enjoy, with enough cameras and film for both of us, with a few hopes and preconceptions, and with a week to do nothing but look and laugh.

It was the first week of March. We hoped for sandhill cranes at Malheur Refuge in the eastern Oregon desert, getting ready to breed and nest, doing their spectacular dance. I knew that there would be thousands of geese and ducks at the Klamath Basin refuges, visiting again on the long annual journey north. I was sure that there would be plenty to see, that an old rule would be proved again: there would be far less of what we expected and a great deal more of what we couldn't anticipate. To live happily with this Law of Beneficent Ignorance, all I need is an open mind, some spare time, and a tremendous amount of film.

Through several counties of northern California, there was a considerable amount of conversation about redwoods, ocean surf, elk, magpies, wine, sunsets, freedom, parents, report cards, and silence.

There was some wonderful silence itself.

There were lectures about ecology, symbiosis, life zones, reforestation, desecration, and self-respect. We searched for perfect house sites (and found at least forty), lichens, agates, gas stations, timberlines, soundlessness, pure air, and communication. We found them all.

"How much virtue there is in simply seeing!"
Thoreau, of course.

Virtuously, Sam observed something simple. Every time we stopped to look at birds, we saw them in profile. They seemed always to be ignoring us, to be looking away, not straight at us. And yet they were able to escape in a hurry when we approached too close. He asked the right questions and got answers, from his own seeing.

He learned, because he saw, that most birds see clearly in two directions at the same time. Watching a bird in profile is watching a bird watching you. In most birds there is also an area of sight where the field of vision of both eyes overlaps, where the vision is stereoscopic, three-dimensional like ours. Flat-faced owls, for instance, see almost entirely that way and so they can hunt in dim light. Some ducks have eyes placed so that they have an area of stereoscopic vision both ahead and behind.

So Sam surmised why most of our pictures are wide instead of long, why this book is printed in this shape. All the pictures are representations of the photographer's looking, and of the bird's looking, too. That's almost communication.

Four bald eagles resting

For two days, we mostly drove and looked. Very few pictures, very many wonderful sights: a forest of towering redwoods that ended abruptly at a clean sandy beach where elk wandered slowly between the line of trees and the smashing surf; a heavy snowstorm in a high pass where the sun shone brilliantly; a slow-moving creek cutting through humid green cliffs where the only sound was the loud dripping of water from the moss and vines onto the stream. One evening I exclaimed about what a gorgeous sunset it was.

"Did you ever see an ugly one?" Sam asked.

On the third day, early, we encountered a little miracle: we had driven fast on a good highway through pretty valleys and had seen almost no wildlife. There was no change in terrain when we came up on the familiar brown sign with the flying goose. It announced that we were entering the Lower Klamath National Wildlife Refuge. It was more an explanation than an announcement because its appearance coincided precisely with a population explosion of birds.

Within fifty yards of the boundary, within a few seconds of our crossing, the apparently lifeless landscape was filled with big and busy life. There was a hawk on every power pole, flocks of coots wandering nonchalantly on the road, resplendent pheasants every few feet in the weeds along the highway, hundreds of pintails and mallards and widgeons in unfrozen patches of marsh and, on the shimmering white ice, crowds of sleeping swans.

Sam and I debated happily whether the birds knew how to read the sign while we readied our camera gear, in touch with no other person but engulfed by life.

For a day and a half, Bob Watson, the refuge manager, drove us around Lower Klamath and Tule Lake, arranged discoveries, encouraged emotional outbursts, and made Sam and me think we were finding things on our own.

Somehow he found us eagles to find. He let us discover that a single night had changed the population of visiting geese from a few to a multitude. He subtly suggested that the birds of winter are the color of winter.

From that, we found that nearly every bird we saw was white or gray or black or some beautiful combination of those neutral shades. The vivid impressions were caused by shapes and sounds and movements.

A resting golden eagle watching ducks

Sam

Whistling swans

Pintails and Canada geese and (opposite) whistling swans

But the great discovery was Sam's. For a couple of hours, we watched flocks of ducks and geese and whistling swans and only he noticed a mathematical wonder: each small group was composed of an even number of birds!

They were choosing each other, pairing, committing, and announcing pictorially that spring was here.

Through three visits to his refuges, Bob Watson had
learned of my inordinate affection for snow geese.
Unerringly, he drove us from pond to field to marsh to
river where we could burn up film photographing the
birds I've photographed most. Strong and clean and
gleaming in the sun, they glimmered and shook
and formed patterns that changed and yet improved
every second.

There were thousands of snow geese there that day
and, in his thirteen years of living with me, Sam had
never seen me more exultant. The delight was
contagious.

Snow geese

Ruddy ducks

In the 250 miles between Tule Lake, California, and Burns, Oregon, there were no snow geese. There was a wonderful, empty highway and a desert that seemed to hold all the colors but no wildlife. The silent shades of tan and brown and gray and purple were gorgeous and it was a splendid relief from all the movement and vivacity of the bird-filled skies of the refuges. It was possible to find a peculiar relaxation at ninety miles an hour.

Sam was enchanted by silver skies and tumbleweeds. We speculated on how long we could stay alive among the greasewood and sage (if there were no automobiles or roads), whether there was something more edible than juniper berries, why there were so many tumbling streams and so few things green. He defined freedom as the feeling he'd have by walking a very long straight line across this cold desert. And agreed that all the loneness somehow translated itself into the strength he'd need to try freedom.

Trumpeter swans

For a full day, we drove over frozen, rutted roads through an awesomely empty high desert in the Malheur National Wildlife Refuge. It was filled only with promise: John Scharff, the refuge manager, pinpointed every nesting site and feeding place he'd memorized in thirty-six years there. His assurance that they'd soon be used again was convincing.

Frequently he'd brake suddenly because, behind a line of bent and icy reeds or a glassy clump of cedar, he'd noticed some swans or geese or a freshened owl's nest. Again, everything was black or white or gray. And, again, all the birds appeared in even numbers. All the world seemed ready for spring, all the birds found themselves paired, everything was getting ready to try again.

Some of the pairs were rarities: trumpeter swans, the world's biggest waterfowl, once down to seventy individuals, now up to a few thousand and off the endangered list because of the security of the refuge system.

Trumpeter swans

And the greater sandhill cranes, a subspecies that numbers only about 3,000, most of them nesting at Malheur. The first couples had come north, but it was too cold and too windy for them to dance. Their day was filled with eating to fuel them against the demanding weather and to prepare them for mating.

And in a grove of spruces where they'd nested for years, there were two great horned owls who were considerably less excited by us than we were by them.

Great horned owls

The next day our guide was Eldon McLaury, the refuge biologist. He took us to another part of the refuge, more desolate, more open, very dry and windy. We bounced over brown rocks, through gray sage to the edge of a frozen lake. Three or four hundred yards away, near the far shore, like lumps of vanilla ice cream on top of the ice, was the biggest flock of snow geese I'd ever seen. All of them, several hundred, were asleep. Around them were whistling swans and trumpeters and a great many pintails and widgeons.

Sam and I set up our long-lensed cameras and Eldon volunteered to work around behind the geese to scare them into photogenic activity. It took him a half-hour to get there; he had to suffer a chill by taking off his bright red vest to wave at the birds and the results were unimpressive. The skittish ducks and the more ponderous swans flew away. The geese awoke and winged a few yards, but the pictures weren't worthwhile. Eldon gave up and began his hike back through the rough tules and willows.

Without any presuggestion, a military jet on some maneuver roared low over the lake. The ugly violation of the wilderness was just what I needed: startled by the hideous noise, the 3,000 geese exploded directly past my camera. The result became the cover of this book.

We had about three hours left before our deadline for leaving the refuge to start the long drive west to Portland. Eldon knew a golden eagle's nest where he'd seen two eggs.

He took us to the base of a yellow mesa. The enormous nest was just below the lip of the cliff, 200 feet above us, built sloppily but efficiently into a rugged niche. As we got out of the car to plot and hope, a magnificent eagle flew up to it, veered away, and disappeared without a sound.

Eldon knew that the bird would not leave the eggs to the dangerous chill and would certainly return to warm them despite our being there. We had only to wait.

The angle was good, the light was perfect, and a picture was a certainty. We set up cameras, ate sandwiches, talked about Waterloo, Iowa (Eldon's home town), and discoursed happily about patience, frustration, wisdom, visual acuity, and the perverse wiliness of golden eagles.

After more than an hour, impatient Sam fixed Eldon's telescope on the nest and asked what the blue thing was on the edge. Eldon thought it looked like a piece of horn or bone. Sam looked again and announced it was the eagle's bill because the brown thing just above and to the left had blinked at him. He was right, of course. It was the female incubating and buried in the huge nest. The other flying eagle must have been her mate, visiting, inspecting.

It was decided that I would stay at the camera and the two younger members of the party would climb the escarpment and look down on the nest. If that scared her away, I'd get pictures and they'd photograph the nest.

They started up and, after they'd gone about ten steps, the eagle flapped out of her nest and away and I got no pictures. She soared out of sight while they continued to the top from where they also got no pictures.

But with her incredible eyes, she must have watched our movements. As soon as the two explorers were off the mesa and down with me, she reappeared low in the sky near the cliff.

She spiraled down, suddenly folded her immense wings against her body to plummet toward the cliff, then spread them quickly to drop softly onto the edge of the nest. She stood there while I made ten identical portraits and then she sprawled into the nest, hidden except for a pale blue bill and a beautiful brown eye.

The talk then was of wildness and the importance of experiencing it, of unpredictability and the value in admitting ignorance, of the mysteries of ecology and the need to feel so we can know what to save, of the virtue in simply seeing.

We were three happy men.

We made some elaborate plans involving half a million nesting birds, some days in the springtime marsh and Eldon and Sam and me. Then to Portland and an airplane home for Sam.

Shortly after he left, I gave a speech to a convention of conservationists on "The Role of Commercial Television in Acquainting the Public with Environmental Problems." The closing line to those professionals was, "There is a sense of mission we should share: we have nothing less than a world to save and it won't be easy or cheap. But we have to keep telling the people."

Maybe one at a time.■

Acknowledgments

There is some kind of wonderful intelligence network that connects all the places of the National Wildlife Refuge system. Because of it, this book was not only made possible but also pleasurable to produce.

If they know you at Okefenokee, they've somehow heard about you at Lower Klamath, too, and there's an enormous amount of hospitality waiting. The people who run the refuges have been unfailingly friendly, dedicated, tireless and tolerant and have extended the ultimate courtesy of passing my name around the network with no warning to either man or bird. Outstanding among them have been these who, while they entertained and educated, also piloted me in trucks, cars, motorboats, airboats, airplanes, and along beautiful foot paths: Lloyd Gunther, Bear River, Utah; Dale Coggeshall, Brigantine, N.J.; J. C. Appel, Chincoteague, Va.; Eugene Kridler, Hawaiian Islands; Robert Watson, Joe Welch and Ed O'Neill, Tule Lake, Calif.; John Scharff and Eldon McLaury, Malheur, Ore.; Harold O'Connor, Lawrence Wineland and James Baker, Merritt Island, Fla.; Keith Hansen, Muleshoe, Texas, and Larry Calvert, Neb Bowen and Jewett Hall, Okefenokee, Ga.

Some of them have moved around or retired since they helped me in those places. So have two of their Washington colleagues: John Gottschalk, former director of the Bureau of Sport Fisheries and Wildlife, and Keith Hay, formerly in the Bureau's branch of conservation education. Both were outstandingly helpful.

I am grateful, too, to Dan Saults, head of conservation education in the Bureau, who has encouraged and helped enormously and has, I suspect, operated that network for my benefit.

A critically important contribution was made by my boss, Reuven Frank, president of NBC News. With surprising ingenuousness, he always acted as though he believed I really did have to go to those peculiar wild places on company business. Also, he arranged for my use of quotations from NBC broadcasts.

I am grateful to those friends who made those quotes: David Brinkley, John Chancellor, Chet Huntley, Douglas Kiker, Jack Perkins and Sander Vanocur.

Joe Delgado of Berkey K & L Custom Laboratories and Alex Rota of Fishkill, N.Y., took extra pains in making the prints and they deserve my admiration and thanks.

So do Margaret Dodd of Scribners, who designed the book, and the remarkable Norbert Slepyan, who edited it, nourished it and never stopped working on it in many peculiar ways.

He even helped pole the boat through the Okefenokee.

R.N.